Behind the Glamour

BEHIND [THE] SCENES
FILM CAREERS

Danielle S Hammelef

raintree
a Capstone company — publishers for children

Raintree is an imprint of Capstone Global Library Limited, a company incorporated in England and Wales having its registered office at 264 Banbury Road, Oxford, OX2 7DY – Registered company number: 6695582

www.raintree.co.uk
myorders@raintree.co.uk

Text © Capstone Global Library Limited 2017
The moral rights of the proprietor have been asserted.

Editor: Alison Deering
Designer: Heidi Thompson and Kayla Rossow
Picture reseacher: Pam Mitsakos
Production specialist: Tori Abraham
Originated by Capstone Global Library Ltd
Printed and bound in China

ISBN 978 1 4747 3814 9
20 19 18 17 16
10 9 8 7 6 5 4 3 2 1

British Library Cataloguing in Publication Data
A full catalogue record for this book is available from the British Library.

Acknowledgements
We would like to thank the following for permission to reproduce photographs: Alamy: Moviestore collection Ltd., 54; Getty Images: Brad Barket, 11 top left, Dan Kitwood, 56, top right, Hero Images, 25 top left, Irfan Khan, 57, Jupiterimages, 26 middle right, Lilly Roadstones, 16 top left, Xavier Arnau, 24 top right; Newscom: FOX SEARCHLIGHT PICTURES/Album, 15, Karl-Josef Hildenbrand/dpa/picture-alliance, 43, 46, Tony Bock/ZUMA Press, 45 middle right; Shutterstock: 9387388673, 6 top right, Aaron Amat, 34 top left, Aaron Lim, 50 bottom right, Africa Studio, 17 bottom, Aila Images, 60 top right, Alex Emanuel Koch, 38, Andrey_Popov, 25 middle right, antb, 21 top left, arek_malang, 49 bottom right, bikeriderlondon, 31 middle right, Darrin Henry, 37 top right, Dean Drobot, 45 top right, DJ Mattaar, 28, Don Mammoser, 7 top right, Gaagen, 44 bottom right, Galushko Sergey Alekseewisch, 22 top right, Gelpi, 37 top left, Golden Pixels LLC, 35 top right, Golubovy, 19 top left, goodluz, 22 bottom right, g-stockstudio, 8, 18, 20, 24 bottom right, 52 bottom right, hangingpixels, 35 top middle, ibreakstock, 26 top right, imging, 34 bottom right, Ivan Cholakov, 59, Ivan_Sabo, 6 top left, Jacob Lund 16 bottom right, javitrapero.com, 4, Jerome Kundrotas, 21 bottom, jgolby, 9 top right, Joe Seer, 12, 13, Karramba Production, 52 top left, KPG Payless, 60 left, Kzenon, 11 bottom, Lilyana Vynogradova, 41 middle right, Linda Moon, 61, LOFTFLOW, 52 middle left, Looker_Studio, 19 top right, MAD_Production, 5, Mark Poprocki, 22 middle right, Mayskyphoto, 40 bottom right, Mazan Xeniya, 1, michaeljung, 30, mikecphoto, 44 middle left, MilanMarkovic78, cover top middle, Milles Studio, 24 middle right, mimagephotography, 37 top middle, Monkey Business Images, 23 middle right, Northfoto, 33 top left, Pavel L Photo and Video, 39 top left, 40, middle right, 44 top left, PedkoAnton, 41 top left, PHILIPIMAGE, cover bottom, racorn, 35 top left, 36 middle left, Rawpixel.com, 10 middle right, 29 bottom left, Razvan Ionut Dragomirescu, 55, Riccardo Piccinini, 17 top left, Rido, 10 middle left, Samuel Borges, 36 top left, SpeedKingz, 17 top right, Stephen Coburn, 33 bottom left, Stock image, 36 bottom left, stocklight, 48, Sue Stokes, 29 middle left, swinner, 42 bottom left, Terence Walsh 31 middle left, VisionDive, 42 bottom middle, Vitalii Nesterchuk, 42 bottom right, Vlad Teodor, 7 top left, wavebreakmedia, 19 top middle, 32, 50 top left, 58, Woraphon Nusen, 42 middle right, Yeko Photo Studio, 6 bottom right; Thinkstock: dolgachov, 49 top left, HASLOO, 53 top right

Design Elements: Shutterstock: Africa Studio, cobalt88, Flas100, igor.stevanovic, Kristina Postnikova, helen-light, optimarc, pan_kung, pashabo

Contents

The clapperboard reads:

PROD. NO.

SCENE   TAKE   ROLL

DATE   SOUND

PROD. CO.

DIRECTOR

CAMERAMAN

INTRODUCTION

On the big screen

Are you one of the millions of people who flock to the cinema each week? Maybe you love cheering for your favourite superhero as he or she battles to save the world from destruction. Maybe you race along with the speeding fighter jets as they dive and roll through the atmosphere in 3-D. Or maybe you try to solve the mystery before the hero.

A BEHIND-THE-SCENES LOOK AT A BEACH
SHOOT FOR THE FILM *RUTA MADRE*

The best films whisk people away to new worlds and make them feel as if they are part of the action. But what happens on the big screen requires a tremendous amount of work behind the scenes. When most people think about dream jobs in film, they think about the glamorous actors or directors and producers. But if you've ever watched the scrolling end credits, you know that hundreds of people work on every film. These behind-the-scene jobs make the actors' characters larger than life for audiences.

If you're reading this, you are likely more than just a fan of films. You want to be a part of the film business. You want to use your talents and love of film to build a career in the industry. And while the entertainment industry is competitive, the good news is, the career possibilities are endless – from using your creative writing ideas as a scriptwriter or film critic to sharing your love of animals as an animal actor trainer. Each job needs savvy people like you who know there's no business like show business.

CHAPTER 1

Talent agent

When actors are busy performing, they don't always have time to find their next job. That's where talent agents come in. Talent agents make it their business to know everything that's happening in entertainment. They know which actors have been cast in which films. They keep in daily contact with directors and producers so they know what film projects are up next.

It's often said that the difference between an aspiring actor and a working actor is a good agent. As a talent agent, it's up to you to find your clients roles that will further their careers. That involves reading lots of scripts. You must be familiar with available roles and pending projects in order to pitch clients to studios, directors, producers and casting directors. Talent agents must also know their clients' strengths and weaknesses. This knowledge helps determine which casting calls to send clients to. If actors have live performances, agents often attend to get to know their clients better. The actors' experiences help agents select auditions.

At a glance

Also known as: Talent manager
Overview: Talent agents manage the people who make films, in particular actors.
Education: University degree in the arts or business; acting and film classes
Special skills: Good people and negotiation skills, calm under pressure, organized, persuasive and detailed
Salary: £22,460 – £89,140 (and more) with an average salary of £50,380/year; pay is earned based on percentage of clients' income.

A strong agent is also a strong negotiator. After all, it's up to the agent to use his or her film industry connections to negotiate the best deals for clients. For example, an agent may try to get a client a share of the profits from a film's ticket and DVD sales. If shops will sell toys based on the films, agents try to get a piece of the profits from those sales. More money for a client means more money in an agent's pocket; actors pay their agents a percentage of their film deals.

GET IN THE SCENE

Agents need to be persuasive, confident and outgoing. Perfect these skills by:

- Joining the debate team
- Reading and writing persuasive essays
- Practising sales pitches with fundraisers
- Running for student government office (or campaigning for a friend) and convincing others why they should vote for you or your candidate

A large part of an agent's job involves networking. This can be a glamorous perk. Agents attend parties, awards shows, film premieres and other events where famous actors, directors and producers are on the guest list. As an agent, it's important to be outgoing and personable. You must be able to make friends fast, act with confidence and trust your instincts about both people and the film industry. Agents know they need good relationships with people in the film business, so it pays to keep in touch. After all, wouldn't you rather work with a trusted friend than a stranger?

Agents sometimes contact famous actors, hoping to represent them for their next starring roles. They also spend time scouting new talent. They attend theatre performances to check out potential clients. Up-and-coming actors also send CVs and performance clips to agents hoping

to earn representation. In some countries, agents must be licensed to represent actors. In the US agents belong to a union such as the Screen Actors' Guild (SAG), which allows them to represent actors who belong to the union. In the UK, most agents belong to the The Agents' Association and performers belong to a union known as Equity.

EQUITY

More than 40,000 entertainment professionals belong to Equity, the UK trade union for professional performers and creative practitioners. This union represents performers and other artists working across the live and recorded entertainment industry. All kinds of performers can join,

including actors, singers, dancers, voice artists, choreographers, stage management, theatre designers and directors, variety, circus and cabaret artists, models, TV and radio presenters, and supporting artists. Equity represents the entertainment professionals and helps them in their careers. Members pay joining fees and a yearly subscription to stay in the union. In return, the union protects its members' rights to fair pay and working conditions.

To join, performers must prove that they are eligible for membership. To do this they must provide proof that they have held a job in an area of work covered by Equity. The role must be in film, TV, radio or theatre, and can be as an actor, audio artist, dancer, singer, stage management, theatre director or designer, or choreographer. If they have worked professionally overseas in one of these fields, they are also eligible for Equity membership.

Students who are studying drama, dance, singing, music, theatre design or circus arts at higher or further education level (NQF level 2 or above) can join as student members.

CHAPTER 2
Dialect coach

Have you ever noticed how an actor can speak with an impeccable British accent in one film and sound like a native German speaker in another? More than likely they worked with a dialect coach to learn each accent. And if you have a knack for perfecting accents or imitations, this might be the perfect career for you!

As a dialect coach, you will teach an actor how to change his or her speech patterns – and sometimes even body language – to match a character's native language. Dialect coaches work with actors until the actors can speak naturally with the new dialect or accent. When dialect coaches do their job, actors' speech rhythms and body movements make their characters believable and authentic to film audiences.

While training for a role as Amelia Earhart, actress Hilary Swank used dialect coach Tim Monich. "When you're in the scene and you're thinking about the accent, you don't have it," Swank said. "At some point, though, it just clicks, and I can let go then of where my jaw goes and where my tongue should be."

At a glance

Also known as: Accent coach
Overview: A dialect coach helps actors speak in certain dialects or accents.
Education: An arts degree; master's degree in voice studies, speech, phonetics or language; acting experience
Special skills: An ear for language; being able to hear what makes a language, accent or dialect unique; ability to teach this to others; excellent communication skills; patience
Salary: £14,400 – £56,000/year with an average salary of £27,100/year

FIRST-PERSON PERSPECTIVE: DIALECT COACH TIM MONICH

Tim Monich taught Brad Pitt to speak as if he were from somewhere deep in the mountains of Tennessee. He taught Matt Damon to speak as if he were South African. For Hilary Swank's role as Amelia Earhart in **Amelia,** he helped her speak like someone originally from Kansas but who lived near Philadelphia while attending school.

Monich always starts with language lab exercises that require actors to listen to a word and then repeat it. "I'm listening for something slightly off," he says. "It could be the actual vowel, it could be the placement or emphasis, the vocal quality — too nasal, too throaty, too gravelly. It could be too long."

Monich says one of the best parts of his job is the people. "Almost everyone I've gotten to work with is really fun, nice and interesting."

HILARY SWANK IN *AMELIA*

He admits to getting star-struck once in his career when he coached Sophia Loren. "I have enjoyed almost every job that I have had, I have to say. Maybe I'm just easy to please, but the quality of people that I get to work with is pretty extraordinary, so what's not to like?"

Dialect coaches help actors master an accent so well that even locals have trouble determining if an actor is a native speaker. How? First, coaches teach actors how to listen to a dialect to find its patterns. They point out the differences in vowels or consonants compared to the actors' own dialects. Maybe the vowels are longer or shorter. The consonants might be more forceful, softer or even missing.

GET IN THE SCENE

- Study as many cultures and languages as you can. Note their origins, history and dialects. How did the languages change over time?
- Keep notes on languages and learn what makes each language sound like it does. You don't need to speak languages fluently to be able to recognize what language it is.
- Watch films and study the actors' accents. Try to imitate the actors' voices.

But it's not just the sounds that are important. Body language plays a part as well. Coaches show videos of native speakers to help actors find the rhythms of speech. They point out how a native speaker's lips, jaws, tongue, teeth and cheeks move while speaking. Native speakers may drop or tense up their jaws when saying certain words. Their lips may round instead of relax. Maybe their tongues press against their front teeth for certain sounds.

As a dialect coach, you get to give actors homework. You'll tell an actor to practise his or her lines in a mirror in order to see the movement of the mouth. This is helpful since actors' facial muscles may need to learn new movements for new sounds. You might also ask actors to record themselves speaking and then play back the recordings to listen for places to improve.

CHAPTER 3

Screenwriter

What do all films have in common? Every single one starts with a script. Writers get script ideas from all sorts of inspiration. Some are original stories from the writer's imagination. Others may be based on news stories, history, books or even religious or mythical stories. A screenwriter writes the script that becomes the road map for a film. This map contains the dialogue and action that will be spoken and performed by the actors. If you have a gift for envisioning stories in your mind, then scriptwriting might be your ticket to the big screen.

Most scriptwriters work on speculation, which is often shortened to "on spec." This means they write the scripts first and then try to sell them to producers. Whether you've sold previous screenplays or just completed your first one, it's your job as the writer to make a director love it. You'll need to find someone who believes your screenplay will be a success before you see your words come to life on the big screen.

At a Glance

Also known as: Scriptwriter

Overview: A screenwriter writes scripts on which films are based; these works may be original or adaptations from books, news stories or other sources.

Education: A BA in writing or screenwriting; additional film degree is very helpful

Special skills: Excellent creative writing skills and a thorough knowledge of film production

Salary: £23,210 – £91,250/year with an average salary of £48,228/year

Screenwriters often begin with a cast of characters. Knowing your characters' ages, hair colours and places of birth is just the starting point as a screenwriter. Screenwriters spend time watching people around them to understand how and why people act, move and speak. When you give your characters fears, flaws and goals, you'll create characters that make film audiences laugh, cry or clench their fists.

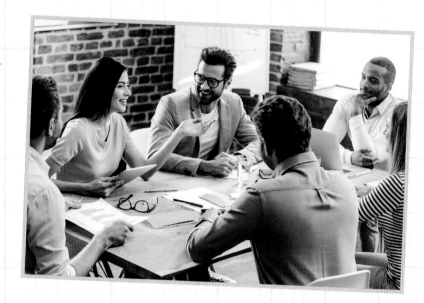

GET IN THE SCENE

- Read — Developing a good screenplay starts with storytelling. What better way to familiarize yourself with stories than to read lots of them?
- Study — Become a good researcher, so that your screenplays are accurate and believable. Also study writing styles — what books make you laugh or cry? Work out why.
- Write — The more you write, the better you will be at it. Try imitating your favourite writers. Write for the school newspaper, or write a play for friends or classmates to perform.
- Attend film festivals — Often you may get to meet screenwriters who penned the films being shown.
- Watch lots of films — comedies, romances, adventure, action, etc. Each kind uses different techniques to set the film's tone. Make note of camera movements, sound effects and music used and dialogue.

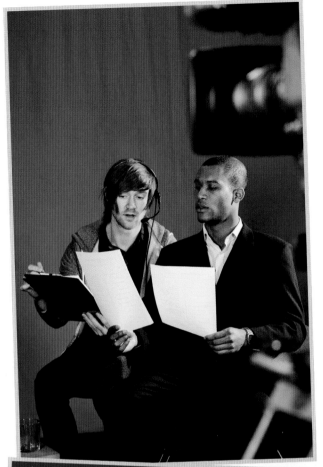

As a screenwriter, you want to *show* the audience what is happening, rather than just *telling* them. You want to create dialogue and action that makes cinemagoers sit on the edges of their seats to find out what happens next. Dialogue must be realistic and believable. Writers include body language cues within the script as a way to add depth to characters. For instance, a character might feel nervous about taking an exam. Adding body language details such as making the character squeeze her hands together, tap her left foot or glance repeatedly at her neighbour's exam paper *shows* the audience how she's feeling.

Once your screenplay is complete, it's time to send it into the film production market. If you have written your screenplay on spec, you'll send copies to film studios and producers, along with a short summary of your script's story. If a company wants to make your script into a film, it will make an offer to buy the screenplay. As the writer, you can then accept, counter, or outright reject the offer.

Once purchased, screenplays become shooting scripts, also called production scripts. In this version of your script, you'll work with the film production crew to add technical instructions, such as film editing notes, camera angles, fade-outs, locations of shots and props needed for every scene.

FAST FACT

Scripts or screenplays must be written in a specific format. They usually have between 90 and 120 pages, depending on the type of film. Shorter films, such as comedies, run around 90 minutes. Dramas run longer — about two hours. How do writers know how long their film script is? They type their scripts using **Courier 12 point font**. One properly formatted script page equals about one minute of screen time. So, a 140-page screenplay will become a 140-minute film.

SCRIPT LINGO

Abbreviation	Meaning
EXT	exterior (outside) setting
INT	interior (inside) setting
I/E	interior/exterior
OS	off-screen
DISS	dissolve shot
F/I	fade in

CHAPTER 4

Casting director

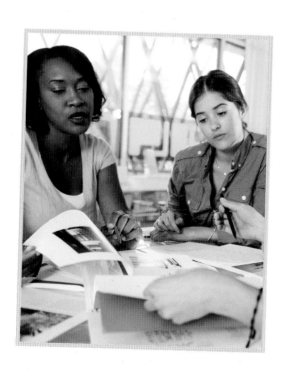

Matching the right actors with leading roles in films can be the difference between a hit film and a box-office flop. That's why directors, producers, studios and film production companies hire casting agents. Like talent agents, casting directors keep up-to-date with the acting world. They know which actors starred in certain films and what roles actors have performed best and worst. An extensive knowledge of films – along with good instincts – helps casting directors decide who would do well in upcoming roles.

Casting directors rub elbows with film stars, directors and producers. To do this well, you'll need to have an outgoing, friendly personality. Those qualities will help you build relationships with people in the film industry.

As a casting agent, it is your job to hire the actors who will appear in a film. First your director will send you the script to read. Then you'll meet to discuss the director's and producer's visions for the leading and supporting cast. Following the meeting, you'll get to work breaking down the script into scenes. You'll take notes on what characters are in each, their traits and how many lines they speak. Then, you'll combine the director's creative vision of each character with your script notes to write character profiles. Then the search is on to find the perfect cast.

Casting agents need to be choosy. That means studying tons of data to find the right actor for a part. Casting directors spend a large amount of time researching portfolios, websites and files. They check out hundreds of photos and CVs of possible actors. They search for undiscovered talent by attending plays, going to comedy clubs and watching small-budget films.

At a glance

Also known as: Casting agent

Overview: A casting director decides what roles need to be filled for scripts and finds, auditions and hires actors for films.

Education: A degree in film studies or acting or a degree in business and communications

Special skills: Knowledge of SAG–AFTRA and Equity rules and how to hold auditions; excellent networking and teamwork skills; organized

Salary: £25,440 – £145,510+ (and more) with an average salary of £54,780/year

Sometimes a director may provide an actor wish list for a film. As a casting agent, it's up to you to contact each actor's agent to see if an actor is available and interested in reading a script. If the actors want to perform in the film, you'll negotiate their contracts with their agents.

Casting directors may also hold open casting calls and organize formal auditions. During casting calls, casting agents and directors listen to actors read parts of the script or watch actors perform rehearsed scenes designed to showcase their talents. Once the team selects the best actors, the casting agent gets to break the good news to an actor and his or her agent.

GET IN THE SCENE

Casting directors know how to spot talent.

They also know the film industry and how to build relationships with actors, agents, directors and producers. Here are some ideas for you to get started:

- Attend film festivals. You may meet actors, directors and producers of featured films.
- Watch films and think critically about actors. Would you have cast any characters differently? Why or why not?
- Help cast a school theatre production. Volunteer to read the script, summarize the characters needed, write the casting call and sit in on auditions.
- Get involved with school or local theatre productions. Gain experience by acting in or producing shows (set design and construction, light and sound crews, etc.).

AUDITION NOTES FOR *THE GREATEST FILM EVER*

AN EXAMPLE OF CASTING DIRECTOR NOTES AFTER AN AUDITION

Girl #1:

- friendly personality
- has experience in university theatre
- well-prepared with monologue for the character she was auditioning for
- had trouble with American accent
- showed a passion for the film and character

Boy #1:

- university student
- monologue was really short
- forgot his lines and stumbled over words
- has acted as an extra in a few films
- when asked why he wanted this role, he didn't give a concrete answer

Girl #2:

- 25 years old — perfect age for character
- fun, outgoing personality
- has a degree in filmmaking
- gave an emotional monologue showing an acting range needed for this film
- very passionate about this film and acting as a career
- came with references from previous directors

Boy #2:

- 19 years old
- outgoing and friendly personality
- acted as lead in several university and local theatre productions
- demonstrated singing and dancing ability that ties to the film's character
- didn't come prepared with a monologue, but read well from the script
- accent needs work

Girl #3:

- good audition; well-prepared
- friendly personality, though quiet
- university degree in education
- acts in local theatre
- has the look we're seeking

Boy #3:

- conceited and aloof personality; may prove difficult to work with on set
- great American accent
- late for audition; claimed traffic was bad
- has the look we're seeking

CHAPTER 5

Location scout

Have you ever wanted to visit a tropical island you've seen in a film? Or maybe you've wondered how a director found that underwater ocean cave or those lush, green hills surrounding an ancient castle? They probably used a location scout. And if you love to travel and explore destinations off the beaten track, this just might be the career for you.

Before a location scout heads out to explore the world, he or she must first read through the script and make a list of all settings needed. Then the scout meets with the director and production crew to create a wish list for film locations. Does the director want a long, winding road lined with forests? Does one scene call for haunted houses and another take place in a busy airport? With production notes in hand, the location scout then goes out and finds the real places that match the film settings.

As a location scout, your packing list should always include your camera and notepads. Scouts snap location photos from all angles and at different times of day and night. This helps the art directors and camera operators determine what the lighting is like. They explore the surrounding locations. Are there noisy airports, highways or industrial factories that will create unwanted noises for the film? Or maybe a residential neighbourhood or school is nearby, making the explosion scenes impossible.

Films have multiple settings, and a location scout has to find them all. Sometimes real-world settings need to be changed to suit the film. Changes may be large, such as paving or building roads, or small, such as removing a satellite dish or changing a shop sign. Even if a location doesn't require changes, scouts must get written permission to use the locations. Scouts need to have outgoing, friendly personalities to build good relationships with the people in charge. If a scout can prove to the local people that he or she is trustworthy and responsible, it will make the job easier when crews are setting the scenes and filming the action.

GET IN THE SCENE

- Watch lots of films and look for stunning settings. Keep an eye out for locations you think are comparable.
- Take landscape photos from different angles and at different times of day.
- Make notes of different locations — what types of films work there?
- Keep a digital photo book of your research.
- Take photography classes or read books and watch videos on photography.
- If you take trips, bring along your camera and notes to start your location files.

Once filming begins, scouts become location managers. In this role you'll be first on set and last to leave. You'll be the go-to person if problems arise. The location manager rents equipment such as electrical generators. He or she arranges tents or trailers for the make-up and hair teams and orders meals for the actors and crew.

At a glance

Also known as: Location manager
Overview: Finding the right place to film scenes for a film; obtaining permission to use the locations; managing locations once filming begins
Education: University degree in film or fine arts
Special skills: Efficient at research; persuasive; communicates well; good at photography; team player
Salary: £24,880 – £106,760/year with an average salary of £51,520/year

CHAPTER 6

Script supervisor

Picture this scene: A man in a red shirt is sitting down at a table to eat dinner with his family. The camera cuts away, and you see one of the children slipping two of her five Brussels sprouts into her lap. The camera cuts back to the man – his shirt is now blue. The view switches back to the girl who just got caught hiding her unwanted vegetables. You notice the sprouts on her plate have doubled.

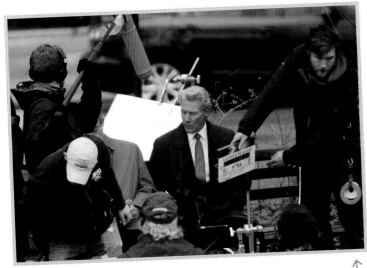

ACTOR RICHARD GERE ON THE SET OF *ARBITRAGE*

Continuity errors such as these sometimes happen in films. So whose job is it to keep track of these details? That task falls to the script supervisor. If you're the kind of person who has a keen eye for details, this behind-the-scenes film career might be for you.

GET IN THE SCENE

Script supervisors need to pay attention to the tiniest details. Here are some ideas you can try now to see if this career is for you:

• Carefully watch films, and pay attention to details. Did you find any errors or inconsistencies? Sometimes watching a film frame-by-frame will reveal mistakes.

• Volunteer for school productions or local theatre to take detailed scene notes (or just try this on your own) during rehearsals. Make notes on characters' clothing, props, locations of everyone and everything, the lighting, etc.

• Take photos. Cameras are essential for a script supervisor's job.

• Practise your note-taking abilities; you must be clear, yet brief, and well organized.

• Play memory skills games — card-flipping match games and number sequences are good examples.

One of the most crucial tools a script supervisor has is a continuity binder. This is where you'll keep track of the details from every scene. A script supervisor also carries a stopwatch to time every take. You'll add these times to your notes. You'll also need a copy of the script. As continuity coordinator, it's your responsibility to cue actors when they forget their lines, so you read along as the scenes unfold.

CONTINUITY BOOK

As a script supervisor, you'll carry a continuity book everywhere on set. This is where you'll write notes about each take for every scene. The book is filled with detailed notes on:

- Actors' wardrobes, actions, lines, hair and make-up, positions and locations in the scene and props they are holding
- Camera angles and lenses used
- Timing — was the scene shot in slow motion, freeze time, normal or fast forward?
- Focus changes — when did the cameras zoom in and out?
- Setting details, such as time of day, artwork on the wall and furniture arrangements

At a glance

Also known as: Continuity coordinator
Overview: Keeps track of the different takes during shooting and takes detailed notes for the director and editor
Education: High school graduate or degree in communications or film
Special skills: Detail-oriented — able to observe and record the smallest things; good communicator; organized
Salary: £20,250 — £75,740/year with an average salary of £55,420/year

Continuity coordinators also keep a digital camera handy. Photos capture details you may not have time to write down in your binder. You'll snap hundreds of photos to help you recall details when it's time to reset scenes for additional takes. These photos can be crucial to re-creating scenes, since shots of the same scene can be taken days or weeks apart. And most of the time, scenes are shot out of order based on factors such as weather, location availability or actors' schedules. Sometimes the ending of a film is filmed months before the beginning!

When filming is finished, the script supervisor isn't done. Now it's time to put on your editing hat to piece together the director's favourite individual takes. Your notes will help organize and combine the takes into a completed film.

SCRIPT SUPERVISORS KNOW EVERYTHING

What might a script supervisor need to know? Check out some examples of questions that might need to be answered behind the scenes:

- Hair stylist: "Was she wearing the red or pink headband?"
- Make-up artist: "Was she crying in this shot?"
- Actor: "Was my shirt buttoned?"
- Dolly grip: "On what word does she cross to the window?"
- Best boy: "What's the cue to raise the lights?"
- Actress: "Do I have my left knee crossed over my right? Or right over left?"
- Prop master: "Was the window open or closed?"
- Special effects: "Is the teapot steaming?"
- Boom operator: "Where was she when she screamed?"

CHAPTER 7

Stunt performer

Film characters flip speeding cars, fall from galloping horses and leap off of high cliffs into swirling river rapids below. They explode through windows or catch fire. How do actors do all of these steal-your-breath stunts that make films so exciting? Most of the time, they don't. When scenes call for dangerous stunts, professional stunt doubles step into the actors' shoes. If you love extreme sports and pushing yourself to the limit, check out what it takes to be a stunt performer.

The best stunts make audiences gasp or hide their eyes because it seems as if there's no way out for the actors. But film stunts only *appear* out of control. In reality, stunt doubles spend hours planning, designing, rehearsing and performing every stunt to make sure it's safe. In your training as a stunt double, you'll learn that safety comes first in every stunt.

GET IN THE SCENE

- Play as much sport as you can.
- Take martial arts lessons.
- Take care of your body. Eat healthy foods, and get plenty of sleep.
- Stay physically fit through dance, horse riding, swimming or other aerobic activities on a regular basis.

At a glance

Also known as: Stuntman; stuntwoman; stunt double
Overview: A stunt person performs the dangerous physical actions that actors cannot or prefer not to do
Education: Athletic training; stunt training; safety instruction
Special skills: Excellent physical condition; excels at several sports and extreme sports; daredevil with knowledge of how to stay safe; acting experience helps
Salary: £683/day or £2,560/week with an average salary of £56,033/year

In stunt school, performers learn how to use safety equipment designed for stunts. For instance, for fire stunts performers wear fire-resistant long underwear or suits, plus gloves and masks. All of it is coated in fire-protectant gel. For car chase or car crash scenes, drivers are highly trained, and cars are equipped with safety harnesses and roll cages. Whenever any dangerous stunt is performed, medical and fire safety crews stand by to help if something goes wrong.

WHAT DID YOU LEARN IN SCHOOL TODAY?

Most stunt performers attend classes at professional stunt schools. These schools train performers how to:

- Fall, flip and then land into air bags
- Use air rams that propel them into the air during explosions on set
- Set up and use decelerators that slow their falls from buildings
- Use wires and cables to create the appearance of flight or levitation.
- Use ratchets that yank performers backwards through the air with attached cables and then land them safely
- Make film fights look real by practising stopping their fists and feet just short of other performers' bodies
- Use trampolines to launch themselves into foam pits and crash mats
- Crash through windows made of safety glass
- Fall down stairs
- Safely perform fire stunts

Before you can ever jump off a skyscraper or fly through the air after an explosion, you'll need to be in top athletic shape. Physical fitness not only reduces your risk of injuries, it also gives you the strength and stamina to perform physically demanding stunts. Stunt doubles prepare for their careers with years of experience in extreme sports, such as high diving, bungee jumping, drag racing, scuba diving, skydiving or rock climbing. They also learn martial arts, boxing and gymnastics. Some even earn pilot's licences, all before ever working on a film set.

FIRST-PERSON PERSPECTIVE: STUNT WOMAN ZARENE DALLAS

A HORSE RIDING STUNT IN ACTION

For as long as Australian-born stunt performer Zarene Dallas can remember, she has wanted to ride horses in films. Dallas's love of riding led her to stunt work. "Now I get paid to hang off a horse, walk through fire or climb up the side of a building," she says.

Dallas's skills include car racing, horse riding, kickboxing and being set on fire. Because of her diverse stunt abilities, she is one of the film industry's most in-demand stuntwomen. She has appeared in films such as *Skyfall, Fast and Furious 6* and *Paddington* and has doubled for famous actresses such as Cameron Diaz and Nicole Kidman. "I have been very lucky to have been offered so much work on so many amazing films and shows," she says.

For Dallas, stunt work is a dream career. "My job is so exciting. Every day is completely different. Even if I am just falling down a hole for the day, I still get such an adrenaline rush every time I'm on set performing a stunt. One day I could be riding horses, the next day I could be in a bar fight or racing a motorbike at high speeds. I absolutely love what I do."

STUNT WORK IN
THE UNITED KINGDOM

In the United Kingdom, stunt performers and coordinators must meet certain standards set by the Joint Industry Stunt Committee (JISC) before they can work. Stunt performers must prove they are experts in six or more of the following categories. The categories must fall within at least four groups, and one must be from Group A, but no more than two categories should fall within one group. At least one year's experience is required in each qualification.

- Group A: **Fighting**

    Categories: combat, boxing or a martial art

- Group B: **Falling**

    Categories: trampoline jumping, high diving

- Group C: **Riding and Driving**

    Categories: motorcycles, cars, horse riding

- Group D: **Agility and Strength**

    Categories: gymnastics, rock climbing

- Group E: **Water**

    Categories: scuba diving, underwater work, swimming

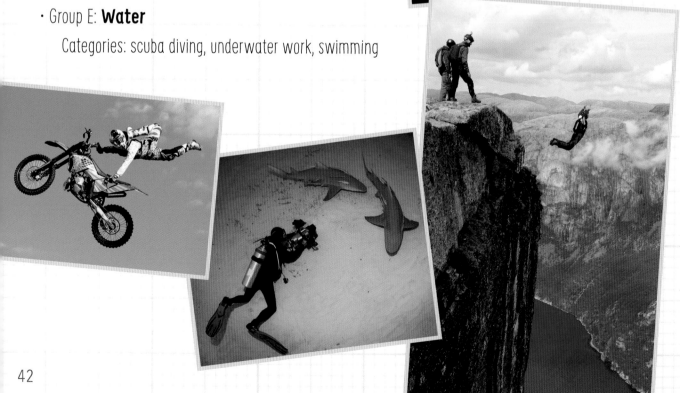

CHAPTER 8

Sound effects designer

Foley artists chop vegetables, smash watermelons, squish cooked chicken and snap celery stalks in half. These artists aren't chefs – they're experts in sound. They use food and other props to imitate or create sounds for films. If you think playing with food and other household items sounds like fun, then the creative career of sound effects designer may be on your play list.

During filming, the sound crew positions microphones to capture the actors' dialogue. This means the background sounds – noises such as clacking horse hooves, swishing clothing, and clicking locks – are not recorded loudly enough. These noises must be added later. It's up to the sound effects designer to re-create these background noises in a realistic way.

Foley artists, named after sound effects pioneer Jack Foley, work in Foley studios to record sounds. Foley studios come equipped with many different floor surfaces, including carpet, linoleum, concrete and sand. Sound designers keep keys to jangle, locks to click and bricks to rub together, just to name a few of their sound effects props.

GET IN THE SCENE

- Listen to films with your eyes closed. What sounds can you identify? What do the sounds you hear tell you about what's happening onscreen?
- Work for your school's radio or TV station.
- Be part of the sound effects team at your local theatre. Learn about microphones, sound mixing equipment and recording equipment.
- Listen and make note of background noises wherever you go. Watch films and listen for similar noises in similar settings. Did anything seem to be missing or unusual?

As part of the sound effects team, you'll watch the unedited film first and note what sounds need to be added and when. Then you create a sound effects cue sheet listing every sound that needs to be re-created for the film. Using your cue sheet for each scene, you and your team then collect the props you'll use to make the sounds. Then it's time to make some noise! As the film plays on a screen in front of you, you and your team switch on the microphones set up to capture your sound effects. On cue, you grab your props to create and record the sounds to match the action.

At a glance

Also known as: Sound effects editor; sound engineer; audio engineer; audio designer; audio artist; sound artist; Foley artist; creative sound designer

Overview: Responsible for sound production and editing; creating and mixing sounds in studio to add sounds to films

Education: A degree in film, music or other arts subject

Special skills: Knowledge of how sounds affect emotions; team player; creative; musical; expert in working sound equipment

Salary: £18,020 – £94,880/year with an average salary of £42,690/year

Sometimes, especially for sci-fi and fantasy films, sound effects designers must create never-before-heard sounds. For instance, you may need to mix different animal noises, such as lions, tigers, elephants and alligators, to create a realistic dinosaur roar. Unusual sound recipes such as squishing jelly in a plastic bag and shaking a bag of popped microwave popcorn may create imaginary alien body sounds when blended together. Need futuristic flying car engine noises? Try recording and blending different aeroplane engine noises. As a sound design engineer, you may slow down, speed up or play sounds in reverse to create new sounds.

FOLEY FOOTSTEPS

One common sound effect needed for most films is footsteps. Any shoe lover who tours a Foley Studio would instantly feel right at home. Foley artists keep all kinds of footwear on hand. It doesn't matter if you're a boy or a girl. Every Foley artist needs to know how to walk in high heels just as gracefully as the actor on-screen. And when an actor's tap shoes click on the wooden dance floor, you'll be matching the beat of their dancing feet step-for-step.

To recreate actors' footsteps, Foley artists first decide what type of surface the actors are walking on. Then they note how fast the actors are walking and if they move with a limp or other unusual gait. If an actor is running barefoot across marble floors or racing down stairs, a Foley artist records bare feet slapping against similar surfaces. He or she might also record feet stomping louder or softer, slower or faster, as seen on-screen. If the actor's boots crunch along a gravel road, you slip on a pair of boots and walk on the studio's gravel surface in time with the actor.

SURPRISING WAYS TO CREATE ORDINARY SOUNDS

DESIRED SOUND	WHAT ARTISTS USE
Horse hooves	Bang two halves of coconut shells together
Fire crackling	Popping plastic bubble wrap
Punching noises	Hitting a phone book or bag of sand
Arrow flyby	Whip a thin stick
Bones breaking	Snap celery
Bats flying	Open and close the umbrella quickly
Chainmail	Rattling set of keys
Dog shaking itself dry	Shake a wet mop
Elephant flapping ears	Flicking a leather jacket
Heartbeat	Press and release a plastic bin lid
Rain on gravel	Sprinkle water on plastic bags
Skiing/ski jump	Slide printer paper over sandpaper or rub printer paper in circles on a desk
Spaceship door opening	Slide a piece of paper out of an envelope
Stone doors moving	Rub two rough stones or bricks together in a slow, circular motion
Unsheathing a sword	Slide a metal baking sheet or spatula off a countertop without lifting it
Vomiting	Squeeze a soaked sponge over a floor or toilet
Bird taking off in flight	Flap a pair of leather or rubber gloves
Rain	Sprinkle rice or sand on a cooking tray
Walking in dry leaves	Crunch cereal flakes
Laser	Hit a tight cable with a stick
Boiling water	Blow into a filled glass of water with a straw

CHAPTER 9

Film critic

Who doesn't love talking about films and sharing opinions about them? Discussing an actor's performance or the special effects can be one of the best parts of watching a film. Now imagine those opinions being published online or in a magazine. And imagine getting paid to do it. Does that sound like your dream job? If so, then you may be the next Roger Ebert.

One perk of being a film critic is being invited to attend screenings. In this career, you'll get to see films before they are shown in cinemas around the world. But being a film critic involves more than just watching a film and sharing your opinion. You must also be a critical and objective thinker in order to evaluate actors' performances and a film as a whole. You must also have strong writing and communication skills to turn your thoughts into a review for readers.

GET IN THE SCENE

- See as many films as you can. Watch them multiple times and try to pay attention to the actors' performances, how the cameras move, the pace of the action and how you felt while watching the film and afterwards.
- Read about films. Learn about different directors' styles and how films are made. The more you know about film, the better you can compare and contrast films.
- Write film reviews for your school paper. Write and submit reviews as a freelance writer for a local newspaper or community newsletter or start a blog.

- Read and watch professional film critics' reviews. What makes a good review? How do they criticize films? Do you agree with their analysis and recommendations?

As a critic, you'll need to watch a film several times before writing your review, focussing on different aspects each time. For example, the first time through, you may take note of how you feel during every scene.

If you attend an early screening, you might observe the audiences' reactions – did they laugh, jump or sigh? Did the audience get the joke or feel the sadness the actors tried to create with their actions and words?

"...after *Days Of Future Past,* you'll be left feeling a little underwhelmed by *Apocalypse,* as there's only so many times that you can watch the world being brought to the edge of obliteration. *X-Men: Apocalypse* still works and entertains, but not quite as emphatically as its predecessors, and it's proof that bigger and louder is not all always better."
– Gregory Wakeman, CINEMABLEND

REVIEWS CAN MAKE OR BREAK A FILM

- "Director Jon Favreau conjures up a magical place to get lost in... *The Jungle Book*, a visual marvel that cuts a direct path to the heart. Favreau, the director of films as diverse as *Elf, Iron Man* and *Chef,* has managed to blend what's best in the jungle stories of Rudyard Kipling and the 1967 animated Disney version into something unique and unforgettable. See it in reach-out-and-touch 3-D if you can, and prepare to be wowed." — Peter Travers, *Rolling Stone*

- "*Alice Through the Looking Glass* ... the design is at once hideous and bland — like a rough draft of a CGI-driven blockbuster that filmmakers would show to studio bosses only to ask for more time and money to create something releasable. There is not a single effect in the movie that stirs the mind, a single composition that stirs the eye, a single line worth remembering." — Matt ZollerSeitz, RogerEbert.com

- "*Captain America: Civil War* ... is equally thrilling, fun, engaging, emotional, smart and thought-provoking, and really everything you want from summer entertainment." — Eric Eisenberg, CINEMABLEND

- "*Star Wars: The Force Awakens* ... It's everything the kid in us goes to the movies for — marvellous adventure that leaves us surprised, scared and euphoric." — Peter Travers, *Rolling Stone*

- "*The Divergent Series: Allegiant* ... plods along like a franchise on its last legs. Who remembers where we left off last time in *Insurgent*? My point exactly — no one... Director Robert Schwentke and his trio of writers haven't given us a single reason to hang around for the last installment, due out next year and laughably called *Ascendant* — ironic, considering the only place the misbegotten series is going is down, down, down." — Peter Travers, *Rolling Stone*

The next several times watching a film, use your knowledge of film and film production to take a deeper look into technical elements. Your readers may want to know if the film's special effects seemed real and believable. You might take a look at the camera techniques the director used. You may also note if camera movements, such as constantly switching point of view, distracted from the action or dialogue.

Now it's time for you to put your thoughts into writing. Cinemagoers rely on reviews to make informed decisions about whether they want to spend their money and time watching a film. A good writer and critic must be able to turn his or her notes into an entertaining, informative review that gives readers an overview of the film without giving anything away.

REVIEWS CAN BE PUBLISHED ONLINE OR IN PRINT MAGAZINES OR NEWSPAPERS

What if you don't like the film? When a reviewer finds flaws, he or she must share these with audiences. Maybe the actors' performances were dull and boring. Maybe the dialogue and writing could have been better. Or maybe the special effects flopped. As the film expert, it's your job to write your reviews objectively. An honest, well-written review will help you earn the trust of film audiences and readers.

At a glance

Also known as: Movie critic; reviewer

Overview: A film critic judges films and makes recommendations about whether or not people should see them.

Education: A degree in journalism, English, broadcasting, theatre or other subject in the arts

Special skills: Excellent writing skills; can work under pressure of deadlines; critical thinking and communication skills

Salary: £25,934 – £88,533/year with an average salary of £47,917/year

CHAPTER 10

Visual effects artist

As you sit in the cinema, ready to watch Spider-Man fly across the screen or animated characters come to life, you have one person in particular to thank – the special effects artist. Instead of paints and canvases, special effects artists use computers and science to make art come alive. They are the ones who make it possible for actors to defy gravity or take on an alien race in another world. And if you're creative and love working with computers, then special effects may be the career for you.

Computer-generated imagery (CGI) is the creation of images and visual effects using computers. Special effects artists use CGI to create characters, environments, objects and spectacular explosion effects. As a special effects artist, you'll use computer programs to create two- and three-dimensional images and models of background scenery and characters. Then, using computer animation, you'll make those images and models come to life.

Filmmakers rely on the work of visual effects artists to help actors do things human bodies can't. For example, an explosion scene might be too dangerous or too expensive to film in real life. That's where visual effects come into play. In the film *Independence Day*, director Roland Emmerich asked special effects artists to destroy the White House on film. He used special effects artists to blow it up again in both *2012* and *White House Down*. To make these explosions happen, a special effects artist must research how these scenarios would happen in real life and use creative thinking to turn them into computer images.

Special effects artists must also be familiar with green screen work. When a scene is impossible to film in real life, actors are filmed performing in front of blue or green screens in a studio. Then it's up to special effects artists to fill in the background, creating the world the director envisions, using a computer. Computer-generated backgrounds are then merged with the scenes filmed in studio.

At a glance

Also known as: Special effects artist, animator, multimedia artist

Overview: A visual effects artist creates special effects for films using make-up, computer graphics, models and camera systems.

Education: Bachelor's degree in special effects, fine arts, or animation

Special skills: Creative thinking, good communication skills, works well under time pressure, excellent drawing and sketching skills, computer programming and graphics skills

Salary: £29,560 – £90,930/year (or more) with an average salary of £51,200/year

A visual effects artist might also work on cleanup duty after the filming is complete. You could use computer-editing software in post-production to erase things that don't belong in the scene, such as cars parked on the street or people peeking though windows. A director might ask you to add animals, trees, or mountains to the background. Or you could use your computer to combine multiple shots filmed on different days or to add actors and props to scenes.

MOTION CAPTURE

Motion capture is one of the most popular CGI techniques used in films. Motion capture – or mocap – involves copying the way a person moves and turning those motions into realistic computer models. Mocap allows filmmakers to create realistic animated characters who move like real people, including showing emotions through facial expressions.

In the 2004 animated film *Polar Express,* mocap allowed actor Tom Hanks to play six roles, including the train conductor, without having to put on make-up or change costumes for each part. Instead, he wore a tight body suit covered with tiny markers that reflect light. As Hanks moved, digital cameras tracked the light reflected by the markers and recorded the motion data. The cameras sent all of the captured data to a computer. Special effects artists then matched his movements to the animated characters.

MOCAP STUDIO ↗

BEST VISUAL EFFECTS
ACADEMY AWARD WINNERS (2000–2016)

2000	*The Matrix*	2008	*The Golden Compass*
2001	*Gladiator*	2009	*The Curious Case of Benjamin Button*
2002	*The Lord of the Rings: The Fellowship of the Ring*	2010	*Avatar*
2003	*The Lord of the Rings: The Two Towers*	2011	*Inception*
		2012	*Hugo*
2004	*The Lord of the Rings: The Return of the King*	2013	*Life of Pi*
		2014	*Gravity*
2005	*Spider-Man 2*	2015	*Interstellar*
2006	*King Kong*	2016	*Ex Machina*
2007	*Pirates of the Caribbean: Dead Man's Chest*		

GET IN THE SCENE

Think you have what it takes to make it as a visual effects artist in the entertainment industry? Here are some things you can do to get a leg up:

- Take computer programming and computer-aided design courses.
- Take drawing courses and other art classes, including film production.
- Watch films and study the special effects. What techniques did the artists use? What effects were convincing or not so believable?

CHAPTER 11

Hollywood's looking for you

From the initial spark that turns an idea into a screenplay all the way up to a film's box-office release, making a film takes hundreds of people working together as a team. Film production offers career choices for almost every talent. Creating a box-office smash demands clever, hard-working people like you who love the film industry and want to be part of the magic films create.

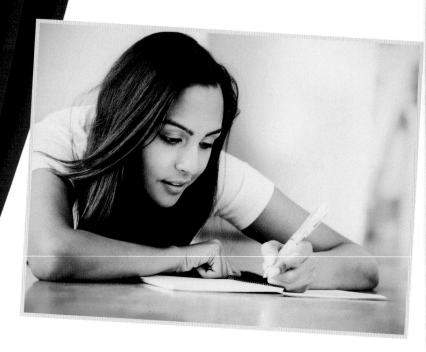

And while actors may appear on the big screen, most people in the entertainment industry work behind the scenes to produce thrilling films for audiences around the world. Even though the writers, dialect coaches, agents and others don't see their names in lights, actors wouldn't be able to wow their fans without talented film professionals like these behind the scenes. Don't be afraid to start small – work as a personal assistant to someone who has the job you want, a runner or someone who does odd jobs around a studio. With passion and hard work, you can work your way into your dream job. One of those behind-the-glamour careers could soon belong to you! Don't keep Hollywood waiting!

FIND OUT MORE

Hatchet Job: Love Movies, Hate Critics. Mark Kermode (Picador, 2014)

Make a Film (Find Your Talent), Jim Pipe (Franklin Watts, 2014)

The Great Movies, Roger Ebert (Broadway Books, 2004)

WEBSITES

www.bfi.org.uk/
Find out more about the film industry in the UK at the British
Film Institute.

www.myfirstjobinfilm.co.uk/resources
Discover more about how to land your first job in film.

www.theguardian.com/film/filmblog/2013/apr/04/most-loved-film-critics
Find out more about some of the world's favourite film critics.

ABOUT THE AUTHOR

Danielle S Hammelef is the author of more than 17 books for children, including the Capstone Blazers Special Effects series on films. She has also written award-winning children's magazine stories, non-fiction articles, poetry and puzzles. Danielle loves to watch animated films and has lost track of how many times she's seen her favourites such as *The Incredibles, Shrek* and *Finding Nemo*. Before becoming a freelance writer, Danielle earned a degree in environmental engineering from Michigan Technological University. Danielle currently lives in Novi, Michigan, United States with her family.

WANT TO LEARN MORE ABOUT THE CAREERS BEHIND THE SCENES IN SOME OF THE WORLD'S MOST GLAMOROUS INDUSTRIES?

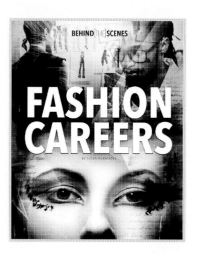

CHECK OUT THESE TITLES TO GO *Behind the Glamour* IN MUSIC AND FASHION.